Push It or Pull It?

written by Rozanne Lanczak Williams
illustrated by Sue Miller

Contents

Push It or Pull It? 2
Index 12

Harcourt

Orlando   Boston   Dallas   Chicago   San Diego

www.harcourtschool.com

How do you make things go?
You add a force–
A push or a pull.
That's what makes things go!

Push it or pull it.
Push it or pull it.
How can I make it go?

3

I'll push the swing
   way up in the air.
When I push it,
   it will go!

Push it or pull it.
Push it or pull it.
How can I make it go?

I'll pull my train
down the railroad track.
When I pull it,
it will go!

Push it or pull it.
Push it or pull it.
How can I make it go?

I'll push my wheelbarrow
  filled with soil.
When I push it,
  it will go!

Push it or pull it.
Push it or pull it.
How can we make it go?

We'll push and pull.
We'll pull and push.
Both will make it go!

When we pushed and we pulled,
We added force.
We got our wagon moving–
We know that's motion, of course!

Index

pull, 2, 3, 5, 6, 7, 9, 10, 11

push, 2, 3, 4, 5, 7, 8, 9, 10, 11